EMMANUEL JOSEPH

Gods of the Game, The Intersection of Sports, AI, and Ancient Myths

Contents

1

Chapter 1 The Genesis of Competition

From the dawn of time, humans have been driven by an insatiable urge to compete. This primal instinct manifests itself in various forms, from hunting and gathering to modern-day sports. The thrill of victory and the agony of defeat are emotions that have been experienced by countless generations, transcending cultures and civilizations. It's within the crucible of competition that the human spirit is forged, tested, and ultimately celebrated.

Ancient civilizations worshipped gods and goddesses who embodied the very essence of competition. In Greece, the pantheon of Olympian gods, led by Zeus, presided over the ancient Olympic Games, where athletes from across the Hellenic world came to showcase their prowess. These games were more than just a test of physical abilities; they were a sacred ritual, a testament to the divine nature of human excellence.

As societies evolved, so too did the nature of competition. The Roman gladiatorial games, the Mayan ballgame, and the Viking battles all exemplified the ever-present desire to prove one's mettle. These ancient contests were not merely for entertainment but were deeply rooted in the cultural and religious fabric of their respective societies. The gods were believed to watch over these events, guiding and influencing the outcomes.

Today, the spirit of ancient competition lives on in modern sports. Whether it's the roar of the crowd at a soccer match or the intense focus of a tennis player, the echoes of the past reverberate through the arenas and stadiums of the present. As we delve deeper into the intersection of sports, artificial intelligence, and ancient myths, we will uncover how these seemingly disparate elements are, in fact, intricately intertwined.

2

Chapter 2 The Rise of Artificial Intelligence in Sports

The advent of artificial intelligence has revolutionized the world of sports in ways that were once unimaginable. From data analytics and performance optimization to injury prevention and fan engagement, AI has become an integral part of the sporting landscape. This chapter explores the origins and development of AI in sports, tracing its journey from a novel concept to a game-changing force.

The early applications of AI in sports were primarily focused on data collection and analysis. Coaches and analysts began to utilize machine learning algorithms to analyze player performance, identify patterns, and make data-driven decisions. This shift towards a more scientific approach to coaching marked the beginning of a new era in sports, where intuition and experience were supplemented by cutting-edge technology.

As AI technology advanced, its applications in sports became increasingly sophisticated. Wearable devices equipped with sensors and AI algorithms began to monitor athletes' physical condition in real-time, providing valuable insights into their health and performance. These innovations not only helped prevent injuries but also enabled athletes to push the boundaries of human potential, achieving feats that were once considered impossible.

Beyond performance optimization, AI has also transformed the way fans engage with sports. From personalized content and interactive experiences to virtual and augmented reality, AI has created new avenues for fans to connect with their favorite teams and athletes. As we continue to explore the intersection of sports, AI, and ancient myths, we will uncover how these technologies are not only enhancing the sporting experience but also connecting us to the timeless spirit of competition that has defined humanity for millennia.

3

Chapter 3 The Modern Gladiators

In today's world, athletes are often seen as modern-day gladiators, revered and idolized for their extraordinary abilities. Just as the Roman gladiators captivated audiences with their strength and bravery, contemporary athletes inspire millions with their dedication, perseverance, and skill. These modern gladiators are the embodiment of human potential, pushing the boundaries of what is possible and redefining our understanding of greatness.

The comparison between ancient gladiators and modern athletes extends beyond their physical prowess. Both are subjected to intense training regimens, rigorous schedules, and the pressure to perform at the highest level. The gladiatorial games of ancient Rome were spectacles of violence and valor, where the stakes were often life and death. While modern sports may not carry the same mortal risks, the emotional and psychological toll on athletes can be equally profound.

In the arena of sports, artificial intelligence has emerged as a powerful ally for these modern gladiators. AI-driven training programs, performance analytics, and injury prevention techniques have become indispensable tools for athletes striving to achieve peak performance. Just as the gods of ancient myths were believed to bestow strength and wisdom upon their champions, AI provides athletes with the insights and guidance needed to reach new heights.

The fusion of human talent and artificial intelligence has created a new paradigm in sports. Athletes are no longer limited by their physical and mental capabilities; they can now harness the power of AI to enhance their performance and extend their careers. As we continue our exploration of the intersection of sports, AI, and ancient myths, we will uncover how these modern gladiators are reshaping the world of sports and inspiring future generations.

4

Chapter 4 The Mythical Inspiration Behind Sports

The world of sports is rich with mythology and folklore, drawing inspiration from the ancient stories that have shaped human culture for millennia. From the heroics of Hercules and the cunning of Odysseus to the wisdom of Athena and the speed of Hermes, these myths have provided a timeless source of inspiration for athletes and fans alike. The tales of gods and heroes serve as a reminder of the extraordinary potential within each of us.

The influence of ancient myths on sports can be seen in the symbolism and rituals that accompany modern athletic events. The Olympic Games, for example, are steeped in tradition and ceremony, echoing the ancient Greek festivals held in honor of Zeus and the other Olympian gods. The lighting of the Olympic flame, the playing of national anthems, and the awarding of medals are all rituals that connect us to the rich tapestry of human history.

In many ways, sports themselves have become modern myths, with athletes taking on the role of contemporary heroes. Their stories of triumph and perseverance resonate with audiences around the world, inspiring new generations to strive for greatness. Just as the myths of old were passed down through generations, the legends of today's athletes will be remembered and celebrated for years to come.

As we delve deeper into the intersection of sports, AI, and ancient myths, we will explore how these timeless stories continue to shape our understanding of competition and excellence. By examining the connections between the past and the present, we can gain a greater appreciation for the enduring power of myth and its influence on the world of sports.

5

Chapter 5 The Digital Oracle

In ancient times, oracles were revered for their ability to provide insights and predictions about the future. These mystics, often associated with gods and goddesses, played a crucial role in guiding decisions and shaping destinies. Today, the role of the oracle has been transformed by the advent of artificial intelligence, which now serves as a modern-day seer, offering data-driven predictions and insights that influence the world of sports.

AI-driven analytics have become an essential tool for coaches, athletes, and sports organizations. By analyzing vast amounts of data, AI can identify trends, predict outcomes, and optimize strategies with unprecedented accuracy. Just as ancient oracles were consulted before important battles or decisions, modern sports teams rely on AI to gain a competitive edge and make informed choices.

The predictive power of AI extends beyond the realm of sports, influencing various aspects of our lives. From financial markets and healthcare to weather forecasting and urban planning, AI's ability to process and analyze data has made it an invaluable resource in navigating the complexities of the modern world. As we continue our exploration, we will uncover how AI, like the oracles of old, is shaping the future of sports and beyond.

While AI's predictive capabilities are impressive, they also raise important ethical and philosophical questions. Just as ancient oracles were often shrouded in mystery and ambiguity, the algorithms that power AI can be opaque and difficult to understand. As we delve deeper into the intersection of sports, AI, and ancient myths, we must consider the implications of relying on AI for guidance and the responsibility that comes with wielding such powerful technology.

6

Chapter 6 The Heroes of the Digital Age

The concept of the hero has been a central theme in mythology for millennia. From Achilles and Theseus to King Arthur and Beowulf, heroes have captivated our imagination with their courage, strength, and noble deeds. In the digital age, a new kind of hero has emerged—one that leverages the power of technology to achieve greatness and inspire others.

In the world of sports, AI-powered athletes are pushing the boundaries of human potential. These modern heroes use cutting-edge technology to enhance their performance, refine their techniques, and achieve feats that were once considered impossible. Just as the heroes of ancient myths were endowed with divine gifts, today's athletes harness the power of AI to transcend their physical limitations and reach new heights.

The stories of these digital-age heroes resonate with audiences around the world, inspiring a new generation to pursue their dreams and strive for excellence. Through social media and other digital platforms, athletes can connect with fans, share their journeys, and offer a glimpse into the challenges and triumphs they face. This newfound accessibility has transformed the way we perceive and celebrate heroism in the modern world.

As we continue our exploration of the intersection of sports, AI, and ancient myths, we will examine how these digital-age heroes are reshaping our understanding of greatness. By drawing parallels between the heroes of the past and the present, we can gain a deeper appreciation for the timeless qualities that define true heroism and the ways in which technology is transforming the world of sports.

7

Chapter 7 The Arena of Data

The modern sports arena is not just a physical space but a digital one, where data flows as freely as the athletes on the field. In this new arena, artificial intelligence plays the role of coach, strategist, and analyst, interpreting vast amounts of information to provide real-time insights and predictions. This chapter explores the transformative impact of data and AI on the world of sports, uncovering the hidden patterns and trends that shape the game.

Data analytics has become a cornerstone of modern sports, providing teams with a competitive edge that was once unimaginable. From tracking player movements and biometrics to analyzing opponent strategies, AI-powered tools offer a wealth of information that can be used to optimize performance and decision-making. Just as ancient warriors relied on the wisdom of their gods, today's athletes and coaches turn to AI for guidance and support.

The integration of AI and data analytics extends beyond professional sports, influencing amateur athletes and recreational activities as well. Wearable devices and fitness apps equipped with AI algorithms offer personalized training plans, performance feedback, and injury prevention tips, making advanced sports science accessible to everyone. This democratization of technology has the potential to revolutionize the way we approach physical fitness and competition.

As we continue to explore the intersection of sports, AI, and ancient myths, we will examine the ethical implications of this data-driven approach. The collection and analysis of personal data raise important questions about privacy, consent, and the potential for misuse. By understanding the benefits and challenges of AI in sports, we can navigate this new arena with wisdom and integrity.

8

Chapter 8 The Deities of Technology

T hroughout history, gods and goddesses have been associated with various aspects of human life, including technology and innovation. In ancient myths, deities like Hephaestus, the Greek god of fire and craftsmanship, and Athena, the goddess of wisdom and strategy, were revered for their contributions to technological advancements. In the modern era, artificial intelligence has taken on a similar role, embodying the spirit of innovation and progress.

AI's influence on sports is a testament to its transformative power. From predictive analytics and performance optimization to fan engagement and personalized experiences, AI has redefined the way we interact with sports. Just as ancient myths celebrated the gods' ability to shape the world, today's technology enthusiasts marvel at AI's potential to revolutionize our lives.

The relationship between technology and mythology is not limited to ancient stories. Modern myths and narratives, such as those found in science fiction and popular culture, continue to explore the impact of technology on society. Characters like Iron Man, who combines human ingenuity with advanced technology, reflect our fascination with the possibilities of AI and its potential to enhance human abilities.

As we delve deeper into the intersection of sports, AI, and ancient myths, we will explore the symbolic significance of technology in our lives. By examining the parallels between ancient deities and modern innovations, we can gain a greater understanding of the timeless quest for knowledge, progress, and excellence that defines the human experience.

9

Chapter 9 The Sacred Arenas

The arenas and stadiums of today are the modern equivalents of the sacred spaces where ancient competitions took place. These venues, whether grand and iconic or humble and local, are hallowed grounds where the spirit of competition is brought to life. They are the theaters where human drama unfolds, where athletes strive for excellence, and where fans come together to witness the magic of sport.

Just as the ancient Greeks held their games at Olympia in honor of Zeus, modern sports venues are often steeped in tradition and symbolism. The architecture and design of these arenas are imbued with meaning, reflecting the cultural and historical significance of the events they host. From the grandeur of the Colosseum in Rome to the cutting-edge design of contemporary stadiums, these spaces serve as a testament to the enduring power of sports.

The integration of AI and technology has further enhanced the experience of these sacred arenas. From smart ticketing and crowd management to real-time analytics and immersive fan experiences, AI has transformed the way we engage with sports. Just as the ancient gods were believed to watch over the games, modern technology provides an omnipresent layer of intelligence that enriches the experience for athletes and fans alike.

As we continue our exploration of the intersection of sports, AI, and ancient myths, we will delve into the role of these sacred arenas in shaping our collective identity. By examining the parallels between the venues of the past and the present, we can gain a deeper appreciation for the timeless nature of competition and the spaces that bring it to life.

10

Chapter 10 The Myth of the Underdog

The myth of the underdog is a powerful and enduring narrative that has captivated audiences for centuries. From David and Goliath to the Cinderella stories of modern sports, the triumph of the unlikely hero resonates deeply with our sense of justice and possibility. The underdog embodies the spirit of resilience, determination, and the belief that anything is possible.

In the world of sports, underdog stories are celebrated and cherished. These narratives capture the imagination and inspire us to believe in the power of perseverance and hard work. Whether it's a lower-ranked team defeating a powerhouse or an unknown athlete rising to fame, the underdog's journey is a testament to the unpredictable and thrilling nature of competition.

AI has added a new dimension to the underdog myth. Through data analytics and performance optimization, AI can level the playing field, providing underdogs with the tools and insights needed to compete against stronger opponents. Just as ancient heroes were guided by divine intervention, modern athletes can rely on AI to enhance their performance and achieve remarkable feats.

As we delve deeper into the intersection of sports, AI, and ancient myths, we will explore the significance of the underdog narrative in shaping our understanding of competition and success. By examining the timeless appeal of these stories, we can appreciate the enduring power of hope and the belief that greatness can emerge from the most unlikely of places.

11

Chapter 11 The Evolution of Sportsmanship

Sportsmanship, the ethical and respectful behavior expected of athletes, has been a fundamental aspect of competition since ancient times. The concept of fair play and respect for one's opponent is deeply rooted in the traditions and rituals of sports. This chapter explores the evolution of sportsmanship, from its origins in ancient civilizations to its modern-day manifestations.

In ancient Greece, the Olympic Games were not only a test of physical prowess but also a celebration of virtue and honor. Athletes competed with integrity, and the games were a reflection of the values and principles upheld by Greek society. The spirit of sportsmanship was considered sacred, and any violation of these principles was met with severe consequences.

In the modern era, sportsmanship continues to be a cornerstone of athletic competition. The values of respect, humility, and fairness are celebrated and upheld by athletes, coaches, and fans alike. However, the advent of technology and AI has introduced new challenges and opportunities for promoting sportsmanship. From instant replays and video assistant referees to AI-driven behavior analysis, technology plays a crucial role in ensuring fair play and ethical conduct.

As we continue our exploration of the intersection of sports, AI, and ancient myths, we will examine how the principles of sportsmanship have evolved and adapted to the changing landscape of competition. By understanding the enduring importance of ethical behavior in sports, we can strive to uphold the values that define true excellence and honor.

12

Chapter 12 The Future of Sports and AI

The future of sports and AI is an exciting and ever-evolving landscape, full of possibilities and challenges. As technology continues to advance, the intersection of sports, AI, and ancient myths will play an increasingly significant role in shaping the world of athletics. This chapter explores the potential future developments and the impact they may have on the world of sports.

One of the most promising areas of AI in sports is the development of personalized training programs and performance optimization tools. By leveraging AI algorithms and data analytics, athletes can receive tailored recommendations and insights that help them achieve their full potential. This individualized approach has the potential to revolutionize the way athletes train and compete.

Another exciting development is the integration of AI and virtual reality (VR) to create immersive and interactive experiences for fans. From virtual stadiums and live-streamed events to augmented reality enhancements, AI-powered technologies are transforming the way we engage with sports. These innovations have the potential to bring fans closer to the action and create new opportunities for interaction and engagement.

As we look to the future, it is essential to consider the ethical implications of AI in sports. From data privacy and security to the potential for bias and inequality, the responsible use of AI is crucial to ensuring that the benefits of technology are realized without compromising the values that define sportsmanship and competition. By examining the intersection of sports, AI, and ancient myths, we can navigate the future with wisdom and integrity, honoring the timeless spirit of competition that has defined humanity for millennia.

13

Chapter 13 The Guardians of Tradition

As sports continue to evolve and embrace technological advancements, there remains a steadfast commitment to preserving the traditions and values that define the essence of competition. The guardians of tradition, whether they are athletes, coaches, or fans, play a crucial role in ensuring that the spirit of sportsmanship, respect, and fair play endures. This chapter explores the balance between innovation and tradition in the world of sports.

In many sports, rituals and customs have been passed down through generations, creating a sense of continuity and connection to the past. From the pre-match handshake in tennis to the ceremonial first pitch in baseball, these traditions serve as reminders of the timeless values that underpin athletic competition. Even as AI and technology transform the way we play and watch sports, these rituals remain a cornerstone of the sporting experience.

The guardians of tradition also include governing bodies and organizations that uphold the rules and regulations of their respective sports. These institutions play a vital role in maintaining the integrity of competition, ensuring that technological advancements do not compromise the values of fair play and sportsmanship. By striking a balance between innovation and tradition, these guardians ensure that the spirit of sports remains true to its roots.

As we continue our exploration of the intersection of sports, AI, and ancient myths, we will examine the role of tradition in shaping the future of athletics. By understanding the importance of preserving the values and customs that define sports, we can navigate the complexities of technological advancement with wisdom and respect for the past.

14

Chapter 14 The Legends of Tomorrow

The legends of tomorrow are the athletes, innovators, and visionaries who are poised to redefine the world of sports. These trailblazers are not only pushing the boundaries of human potential but also shaping the future of competition through their pioneering use of AI and technology. This chapter explores the stories of these modern legends and the impact they are having on the world of sports.

From AI-powered training programs to cutting-edge performance analytics, the legends of tomorrow are leveraging technology to achieve extraordinary feats. These athletes are at the forefront of a new era in sports, where data-driven insights and advanced algorithms are transforming the way they train, compete, and recover. Their stories serve as a testament to the limitless possibilities that AI and technology offer.

The impact of these modern legends extends beyond their individual achievements. By embracing innovation and challenging the status quo, they inspire others to follow in their footsteps and explore new ways of reaching their potential. Their dedication, perseverance, and willingness to embrace change serve as a source of inspiration for aspiring athletes and sports enthusiasts around the world.

As we delve deeper into the intersection of sports, AI, and ancient myths, we will uncover the stories of these legends and the legacy they are creating. By examining their journeys and the impact of their innovations, we can gain a greater appreciation for the transformative power of technology and the enduring spirit of competition that defines the world of sports.

15

Chapter 15 The Timeless Quest for Excellence

The quest for excellence is a timeless pursuit that transcends cultures, generations, and disciplines. Whether in sports, the arts, or academia, the drive to achieve greatness and push the boundaries of human potential is a defining characteristic of the human experience. This chapter explores the enduring nature of this quest and its relevance in the modern world of sports and AI.

Throughout history, the pursuit of excellence has been celebrated in myths, legends, and stories. From the feats of ancient heroes to the achievements of modern athletes, the quest for greatness has always been a source of inspiration and aspiration. This timeless pursuit is rooted in the belief that through hard work, dedication, and resilience, individuals can overcome challenges and achieve extraordinary feats.

In the world of sports, the quest for excellence is embodied by athletes who strive to reach their full potential and achieve greatness. AI and technology have become powerful allies in this pursuit, providing athletes with the tools and insights needed to optimize their performance and push the limits of what is possible. By leveraging AI, athletes can achieve new heights and continue the timeless quest for excellence.

As we conclude our exploration of the intersection of sports, AI, and ancient myths, we will reflect on the enduring nature of this quest and its implications for the future. By understanding the timeless drive for excellence and the role of technology in supporting this pursuit, we can appreciate the profound impact of AI on the world of sports and the timeless spirit of competition that defines humanity.

Book Description

Dive into a captivating journey that intertwines the worlds of sports, artificial intelligence, and ancient myths in "Gods of the Game The Intersection of Sports, AI, and Ancient Myths." This thought-provoking book explores how the timeless spirit of competition, embodied by the heroes and legends of ancient civilizations, continues to inspire and shape the modern world of athletics.

Through twelve meticulously crafted chapters, you'll discover the evolution of sports from its mythological origins to its transformation in the digital age. Learn how AI technology is revolutionizing the way athletes train, compete, and engage with fans, while uncovering the ethical and philosophical implications of relying on data-driven insights.

From the modern gladiators who push the boundaries of human potential to the digital oracles that provide real-time predictions and guidance, "Gods of the Game" delves into the symbolic significance of technology and its impact on the quest for excellence. Explore the sacred arenas where the spirit of competition is brought to life, and celebrate the enduring myths of the underdog and the timeless pursuit of greatness.

Perfect for sports enthusiasts, tech aficionados, and lovers of mythology, this book offers a unique and compelling perspective on the intersection of tradition and innovation. Join us as we honor the past, embrace the present, and envision the future of sports in an era defined by artificial intelligence and the enduring power of ancient myths.